LEGENDS
OF C

Louise Maskill

Published by Bradwell Books
11 Orgreave Close Sheffield S13 9NP
Email: books@bradwellbooks.co.uk

All rights reserved. No part of this publication may be reproduced, stored in a retrieval system or transmitted in any form or by any means, electronic, mechanical, photocopying, recording or otherwise without the prior permission of Bradwell Books.

British Library Cataloguing in Publication Data: a catalogue record for this book is available from the British Library.

1st Edition

ISBN: 9781912060696

Design by: Andrew Caffrey

Typesetting by: Mark Titterton

Photograph Credits: iStock and credited individually

Front Cover: Lanyon Quoit – King Arthur's dining table?

Print: Gomer Press, Llandysul, Ceredigion SA44 4JL

CONTENTS

Introduction	4
Heroes and Villains	6
Witches and the Devil	12
Beasts and Birds	17
Saints, Stones and Curses	21
Piskeys, Giants and Fairies	27
Pools, Rivers and Other Water Sources	34
Mining, Fishing and Other Occupations	43
Superstitions and Omens	52
The Journey Through Life	57
The Wheel of the Year	64
A Cornish Miscellany	75

INTRODUCTION

The folk tales and folklore of the British Isles make for an endlessly fascinating study. The cultural melting pot of ancient Britain has bequeathed us an eclectic mix of heroes, villains, myths and legends, and over the centuries a glorious confusion of beliefs has evolved to account for phenomena both natural and supernatural, and to explain, inhabit and name landscape features such as hills, rivers, woods, chasms, moors and marshes.

Dramatic skies over Bodmin Moor, in the heart of Cornwall.
iStock

Our ancestors lived very different lives to those we enjoy today. Most were tied to the land and had intimate relationships with the changing seasons and the natural world. Few travelled further than their local environs and perhaps the nearest market town, but this seemingly limited existence was nevertheless richly coloured with an awareness of another world, where supernatural beings existed just outside mortal awareness, where illness and death could be caused not by germs or viruses but by witchcraft, and where mythical heroes could be brought to life in dramatic stories and legends retold down the generations.

In this book you will be introduced to some of the legends and folklore which enriched the days and nights of the folk of Cornwall in days gone by. You will meet fairies, witches, saints and the Devil, and encounter heroic legendary figures such as King Arthur, Jan Tregeagle, the giant Cormoran and St Michael the Archangel. You will read about smugglers and wreckers, curses, superstitions and omens for both good and bad luck, and the ceremonies and rituals associated with the rural year and critical stages in life, as well as a few particularly Cornish customs and traditions.

Welcome to Cornwall, a truly magical county!

HEROES AND VILLAINS

Tintagel Castle – the birthplace of King Arthur.
Valery Egorov

King Arthur

There are many Arthurian sites and legends associated with Cornwall – perhaps more than in any other area of Britain. The legend of his birth at Tintagel is well known; he was conceived by Ygraine, the wife of Duke Gorlois of Cornwall, when she was visited by the High King Uther Pendragon under an enchantment to make him look like Gorlois. Uther and Ygraine were later married after Gorlois' death in battle, but Arthur's birth was kept secret and Uther's magician, the great Merlin, took him to be raised away from Uther's court.

Merlin knew Cornwall well. He once made a prophecy that an invading force would come ashore at the Rock of Merlin, off Mousehole quay, and would lay waste to the settlements of Newlyn, Paul and Penzance, all in Mount's Bay. The prophecy came true in 1595, when four Spanish galleons came ashore here and burned the towns of Mount's Bay.

The Spaniards' rampage came to end, however, when they approached Penryn and heard the sounds of musket and cannon fire. Thinking the militia had arrived, they fled back to sea – a narrow escape for Penryn, considering that the sounds were part of a battle scene in a play being staged in the town!

Arthur is still thought to hunt in Cornwall; when the wind whistles over Goss Moor, near Newquay, one can hear the notes of his hunting horn as he pursues a deer, and his horse left a hoofprint on a stone near Castle-an-Dinas on the moor. Dozmary Pool, on Bodmin Moor, is thought to be the home of the Lady of the Lake, from whom Arthur received his mystical sword Excalibur and to whom the sword was returned after his death.

Dozmary Pool, on Bodmin Moor. The home of the Lady of the Lake?
iStock

In a final note, it is believed that King Arthur met a bloody end at the hands of his traitorous son Mordred on the battlefield of Camlann, which is thought to lie somewhere in Cornwall – perhaps at Slaughter Bridge, on the River Camel near Camelford, where there is a stone slab known as King Arthur's Tomb which is thought to mark his final resting place. As he died Arthur's soul took flight in the shape of a Cornish chough, a member of the crow family which appears on the Cornish coat of arms along with a miner and fisherman. The bird is black with red bill and feet, thought to symbolise the blood of the battlefield, and a Cornishman seeing a chough will always doff his cap and greet it with the words: "Good day to you, sire."

A Cornish chough. "Good day to you, sire."
iStock

The chough was extinct in Cornwall but has recently returned in small but growing numbers. Let us hope it brings Arthur's soul with it – for as the old Cornish song goes:

> *Where shall we find King Arthur?*
> *His place is sought in vain.*
> *Yet dead he is not, but alive,*
> *And he shall come again!*

Castle Dore, a hillfort near Fowey, is traditionally associated with the story of Tristan and Iseult. Tristan was the trusted and beloved nephew of King Mark of Cornwall, whose court was at Castle Dore. Mark sent Tristan to Ireland to woo the beautiful Iseult on his behalf and bring her home to be Mark's queen, but instead the pair took a love potion and fell madly in love. Iseult married Mark as arranged, but she and Tristan were compelled by the potion to seek each other out, and eventually Mark discovered their affair. He resolved to punish his nephew and his bride, capturing them and condemning them both to death, but they escaped and both left Cornwall – Iseult to return to Ireland and Tristan to Brittany. Years later Tristan was mortally wounded and sent word to Ireland for Iseult to come to heal him, but they were betrayed and Tristan died thinking that Iseult had deserted him. She died of grief when she arrived to find his corpse. Theirs was one of the great medieval romantic tragedies, and in fact the tale may predate Arthurian legend, possibly inspiring the tales surrounding the adulterous love triangle between Arthur, Lancelot and Guinevere.

Jan Tregeagle

One of Cornwall's most infamous sons, Jan Tregeagle, was an unscrupulous man, a lawyer and estate steward who was renowned for being the most evil man ever to have lived in Cornwall. He was widely thought to have sold his soul to the Devil, but as he grew old he began to repent of his many sins and tried to atone by such deeds as donating to the church and the poor, and by attempting to persuade the local clergy to intercede on his behalf and save his soul from Old Nick's clutches.

As he lay dying he tricked or bribed the local parson into burying him in consecrated ground in St Breock churchyard, but he was called forth from his grave by a defendant in court. Just before his death Tregeagle had witnessed this man borrowing a large sum of money from a moneylender, but the debtor later denied all knowledge and refused to pay up. In court the moneylender argued that Tregeagle had witnessed the deal, but since he was dead the debtor believed he was safe. Laughing, he said, "If Tregeagle saw it, he must come forward and declare it!"

There was a flash of lightning and the recently deceased Tregeagle duly appeared, testified against the debtor, but then refused to return to the afterlife, noting quite rightly that mundane reality was far preferable to the torments of Hell where he had been residing since his death.

Tregeagle went on to have many posthumous adventures, pursued by the Devil who felt cheated of the soul of such a notorious sinner. Tregeagle is said to have been bound by a parson to empty Dozmary Pool with a leaking limpet shell, charged with weaving ropes out of sand on the beach at Gwenvor Cove, got drunk with Devil at Lanlivery, and got stuck with his head through a window in the chapel at Roche Rock. He is now damned to wander the moors and coast, howling and roaring his rage and frustration in the teeth of storms and angry seas.

Gwenvor Cove, where Jan Tregeagle was condemned to weave ropes from sand.

WITCHES AND THE DEVIL

Tregeseal stone circle and Carn Kenidzhek – where the Devil staged a wrestling match.
iStock

The Devil is said to be afraid of Cornwall and to avoid it, since he has no wish to be turned into a saint, as seems to happen to many people who cross the Tamar and venture west. Nevertheless, he comes here occasionally to work mischief and cause problems and upset for the local population. He is thought to have held a wrestling match with a band of demons at Carn Kenidzhek, a cairn near St Just, causing some terror to a pair of miners who witnessed this sporting event as they returned home from work late at night. Invited to join the spectators by a mysterious stranger on horseback, the two men watched as a pair of demons fought and grappled. Eventually one was thrown to the ground and appeared to be dying, upon which one of the miners began to pray. Instantly there was a terrible rushing wind, the ground shook, and all the demons rushed hither and thither and then were gone. The terrified miners found themselves lost on the barren land near the cairn and couldn't find their way home until dawn broke.

Towednack Church, near St Ives, has a squat square tower, and local legend suggests that it once had adornments and pinnacles like other churches but the Devil broke them off. Likewise, Satan also is said to have demolished the tower of Egloshayle Church because he couldn't bear the sound of the church bells.

Old Nick is reputed to have left his footprints at the top of an outcrop of rock near Newlyn Church, known locally as Tolcarne or the Devil's Rock. The story goes that he was caught stealing nets from the Newlyn fishermen, and when he was being pursued he tripped and caught his cloven hooves on the rock, leaving the strange markings that can be seen there today.

He is also said to inhabit caves or holes in the ground; one such is Piper's Hole, on St Mary's in the Isles of Scilly. The locals suggest that this hole leads to a tunnel under the sea, which emerges at another Piper's Hole on the neighbouring island of Tresco. In order to test this supposition a dog was once sent in at one entrance; sure enough, it emerged some time later from the other one – but with most of its fur singed off, and carrying a distinct whiff of brimstone.

Cornwall had its share of witches, as evidenced by courtroom accounts of women who were accused of witchcraft by neighbours (who often had some sort of grudge). There were accusations of dancing cats, marks on the body, shape-changing into hares or other animals, or general ill-wishing. However, the craze for executing witches that gripped the rest of the country in the sixteenth and seventeenth centuries doesn't seem to have taken firm root in Cornwall; the worst punishment that most of these accused women received was a short gaol sentence, and many were acquitted.

One witch, Madgy Figgy, lived near Land's End and took great delight when a ship was wrecked; she would sit on a chair-shaped rock on the cliff on stormy nights, watching for an unfortunate vessel and then claiming her share of the spoils that washed ashore. One night, however, she met her match. A ship ran aground in a storm and Madgy found a woman's body adorned with jewels and trinkets, claiming the jewellery as her prize. In the days that followed, however, she was plagued by a light which played around her house and at the place where she had buried the corpse.

A few weeks later a foreigner came to the village and asked to be shown the unknown woman's grave. The locals claimed ignorance, but when night fell the lights led him to the grave and then to Madgy's cottage and straight to the wooden chest where she had stored the jewels. Madgy immediately handed them over, muttering, "One witch always knows another, dead or living."

If someone believed themselves to be under a witch's curse, a common strategy was to consult the local "peller", a white witch or wizard who made a living removing black witch's curses. Pellers might suggest remedies for the cursed person, such as creating a witch-bottle containing the witch's blood, urine, hair or nail

Land's End – where Madgy Figgy watched for wrecks.

clippings, and heating it over a fire. This, so the pellers said, would cause the witch untold agony until she removed the curse.

Local people knew and used their own healing charms for minor ailments. Warts could be healed by rubbing them with a penny and then burying it; within a day or two, so it was said, the wart would be gone. One old Cornish man did this and cured his warts, but a few days later his son announced that he was short a penny for an ounce of tobacco, so he was going to dig up his father's coin. The father warned against this, but the son went ahead anyway – and within a few days his hands were covered with warts.

The Cornish believed firmly in the powers of plants and herbs to heal; medical doctors cost money, and it was usually cheaper and quicker to visit the local herbalist. It used to be said in Cornwall that there was a doctor in every hedge. Plants such as ivy, elder, mallow and nettles were used in various concoctions, sometimes gathered at certain phases of the moon for extra efficacy.

Boscastle, home of the Museum of Witchcraft and Magic.
iStock

One town in Cornwall is particularly associated with witches and witchcraft – the town of Boscastle, on the Atlantic coast near Tintagel. A local girl from St Teath was once renowned for being able to see and speak with piskeys, who granted her all manner of healing powers and the ability to see the future. In more modern times the town of Boscastle has been home to the Museum of Witchcraft and Magic since the 1960s, once displaying the bones of Joan Wytte, a famous seer, healer and clairvoyant from Bodmin who died in Bodmin Gaol in 1813. However, the Museum experienced a series of paranormal happenings while her skeleton was on display, which only ceased when Joan's remains were given a more dignified burial in a peaceful Boscastle wood.

BEASTS AND BIRDS

Like many other areas of the country, Cornwall has its share of spectral black creatures — dogs, cats, sometimes pigs or donkeys — which haunt wild and lonely roads. Sightings of a monstrous black cat have plagued Bodmin Moor over many years; the feline Beast of Bodmin is said to be as big as a calf with eyes like saucers. Tracks have been found at various points and times, cattle and sheep have been killed or mutilated, and a large catlike skull was found (although it was later concluded that this had once been part of a leopard skin rug!). Video and photographic evidence has been recorded, although this is never distinct or irrefutable; it remains unclear whether the Beast of Bodmin is a real creature or something of more supernatural origin.

The Cheesewring, on Bodmin Moor. The haunt of the Beast?
iStock

Unlike in other areas of the country, however, in Cornwall apparitions like the black cat of Bodmin Moor are often thought to be connected with the spirits of miners who have died in accidents underground. A pack of demonic hounds is also said to run howling across the Cornish moors, led by their master in a wild hunt. The hounds are known as the Dandy Dogs, while their master is none other than the Devil himself.

The last wolf in Cornwall was killed near the village of Crowlas, not far from Penzance. Legend says that the creature lived in the local forest for some time and wreaked havoc on farms by preying on sheep and cattle. The final straw came when the wolf took a child; at that point the villagers turned out in force, cornered the creature and killed it. Some say its lonely cries can still be heard echoing across the land.

A white hare may sometimes be seen running towards the Jolly Sailor Inn in Looe. This animal is thought to be the ghost of a young girl who committed suicide by drowning herself, but who now returns to warn of imminent danger to local people. Fishermen in the village would often stay at home rather than putting to sea if the hare had been seen, preferring the loss of a day's catch to the risk of tempting fate.

Puffins, with their striking appearance and endearing habits, have played a significant role in Cornish folklore. It is said that the Blanchminster family, a Norman family who held the Isles of Scilly in the fourteenth century, paid rent to the Earldom of Cornwall in the shape of three hundred puffins annually. It is likely that these birds were eaten, especially since they were literally regarded as fish in the Middle Ages, so they could be eaten during Lent and on other fasting days in lieu of meat. As such, they would have been a valuable addition to the diet.

Puffins.
iStock

Cornish fishermen will not kill gulls as they believe them to contain the souls of drowned mariners. Likewise, anyone who killed a robin or a wren was shunned, and may have been cursed or stunted in growth by the evil deed. The Cornish also held superstitious beliefs about insects, spiders and snails; earwigs were killed at every opportunity, because they were thought to make their homes in people's ears and drive them mad. However, spiders were thought to be lucky, since one had spun a web over the infant Jesus to hide him from the murderous Herod. Ants (or "muryans", in the local dialect) were thought to embody the souls of unbaptised children, but bees were lucky if they swarmed or settled near your house.

One summer evening in 1886, the residents of Redruth became aware of an approaching storm. Expecting nothing more than a summer thunderstorm, they were startled when, along with the more usual fall of rain, a heavy shower of snails fell from the heavens. The downpour lasted around ten minutes, and by the end of it the gastropods lay thick on the ground over an area of about half a square mile. The snails were alive, and were distinctly different from the local varieties – no satisfactory explanation has even been offered, although the event was widely reported in the press at the time.

Finally in this roundup of Cornish animal tales, in a legend which is shared by other locations in the UK (notably Hartlepool), it is said that in 1805 the fishermen of Mevagissey rescued and brought ashore a monkey, which must have somehow survived a wreck at sea. This was during the Napoleonic Wars, however, and the suspicious locals took the creature for a French spy. They put it to the question, but when it refused to yield any information they hanged it. One wonders what state secrets it took to its grave.

SAINTS, STONES AND CURSES

St Michael's Mount.
iStock

It is sometimes said that there are more saints in Cornwall than there are in Heaven. Cornwall's patron saint is St Michael, and there are many examples of Cornish churches dedicated to him, mostly located in high places as befits a building sacred to one of the archangels. Of these, the medieval church atop St Michael's Mount is the most famous, with its castle and small community crowded close on this rocky island in Mount's Bay near Marazion. St Michael's connection with this place is that he once set up watch here for the Devil, who had let it be known that he wanted Cornwall for himself.

Sure enough, one day the Devil appeared, carrying a boulder glowing red-hot straight from the fires of Hell. St Michael immediately launched himself from the Mount and a deadly airborne battle ensued; eventually the archangel was victorious, and the Devil dropped his boulder and fled. The rock landed in Helston and rested for many years in the yard of the Angel Inn; this story is supposedly the origin of the village's name.

St Piran, one of Cornwall's favourite saints, came originally from Ireland in the sixth century. His story goes that his lawless countrymen tired of his saintly good deeds and threw him into the sea chained to a millstone. However, the stone miraculously transformed and became buoyant, and he floated across the Irish Sea and came ashore on Penhale Sands, near Perranporth. He built a tiny church on the beach, known as St Piran's Oratory, but it was later abandoned to the encroaching sands. It has been excavated since then, most recently in 2014, and is currently protected from the dunes by a concrete wall; this tiny chapel is possibly the oldest site of Christian worship in Cornwall, and is remarkably well preserved for a building that is around 1300 years old. Piran is also said to have discovered tin in the local rock near Perranporth and kick-started the local tin-mining industry— but that's another story!

St Ia also came across the sea from Ireland, but she floated on a leaf which had miraculously become big enough to support her, washing ashore at St Ives and giving the town its name. St Neot was a monk and hermit, who once charmed all the local crows and confined them in the enclosure of Crowpound every Sunday so that the local people could attend church instead of having to spend the day in their fields scaring away the ravenous birds. He also persuaded deer from the forest to pull his plough when the oxen belonging to his monastery were stolen by thieves.

Finally in this quick who's who of Cornish saints, St Petroc loved animals and refused to countenance any violence or cruelty towards them. He once charmed a sea serpent that was terrorising the waters around Padstow and persuaded it to swim far out to sea and hunt there, rather than preying on the local fisherman. On another occasion he was visited by a dragon, much to the consternation of the inhabitants of nearby Bodmin. However, the dragon had a splinter in its eye; Petroc was able to remove the splinter, and the dragon flew away, never to be seen in the area again.

The Merry Maidens is the name given to a stone circle close to St Buryan, near Land's End. The circle is associated with a pair of standing stones a short distance away known as the Pipers; legend has it that these were once flesh-and-blood musicians, who agreed to play for a group of nineteen local maidens one Saturday afternoon. The girls danced and the pipers played long into the moonlit night, until midnight rolled around and Saturday turned to Sunday. As everyone knows, dancing and merry-making on the Sabbath are forbidden, and the pipers and maidens were all turned to stone for their sin. Sometimes, however, on a full moon, girls and pipers all revive to play and dance again.

The same story is told of the Nine Maidens, a stone circle at Boscowen Un which is also said to be a circle of girls turned to stone for dancing on the Sabbath. With a slight variation, it is also thought to be the origin of the Hurlers, three concentric rings of stones on Craddock Moor near Minions, north of Liskeard. These stones were apparently once people who decided to continue a game of the Cornish sport of hurling on the Sabbath, and were petrified. Legend states that the stones of the Hurlers cannot be counted, and anyone who attempts this and achieves the same number twice will surely die within the year.

The Hurlers stone circles – once a group of sporting combatants?
iStock

Finally, the medieval cross known as Long Tom, to the south of Minions and not too far from the Hurlers, was thought to be once a poacher named Tom, who accepted a challenge from the Devil to see who could take the most souls in a single night. Tom worked hard and amassed a fine collection of rabbits, deer and fowl, but he was beaten hands down when the Devil turned up at dawn having brought the plague to Cornwall, thereby accounting for more souls than Tom could hope to gather. The Devil took Tom's soul as well, turning him to stone and leaving him on the moor to act as his own memorial.

For some stones in Cornwall the opposite effect appears to happen; these are quite definitely rocks and always have been, but they are said to come to life and move from time to time. The Twelve

O'Clock Stone near Nancledra turns itself around when it hears a cock crowing, while the top stone of the Cheesewring, a striking rock formation near Liskeard, apparently does the same thing. There was once a druid who lived near here, who would sit on a rock now known as the Druid's Chair and offer drinks to passing hunters out of a golden goblet that never ran dry. One hunter accepted a wager to drink all the water in the goblet, but when he was unable to do so he became enraged and galloped off with it. However, his horse threw him at Rillaton and he broke his neck; he was buried where he lay, still clutching the goblet, and a barrow was built over him. Interestingly, when the Bronze Age barrow at Rillaton was excavated a fabulous golden goblet was found; it can now be seen in the British Museum in London, after serving for a while as the receptacle for the collar studs of King George V…

Some stones are associated with saints; St Levan's Stone is a massive cleft boulder in the churchyard of St Levan church. It is said that the stone was once whole, until St Levan, a righteous and holy but somewhat stern fellow, became so incensed by the sinfulness of the local people that he struck the stone a blow with his staff, whereupon it split in two. He then prophesied that on the day when a loaded packhorse could pass through the cleft in the stone, the world would end. It is to be hoped that the locals keep a close eye both on the stone and on any loaded packhorses who happen to be wandering nearby.

Finally in this section, Men-an-Tol, in Madron parish near Penzance, is a holed stone set upright on its circumference between a pair of other stones. It has long been thought to have magical properties; children passed through the hole in the centre of the stone would be cured of scrofula or rickets, crawling through the stone is said to alleviate back and neck problems, and it also has fertility associations.

Men-an-Tol, in West Cornwall.

PISKEYS, GIANTS AND FAIRIES

Cornish piskeys were mischievous spirits of natural places – woods, caves, rivers or hills. They took delight in "mazing" travellers into losing their way; someone who is lost is still said to be "piskey-led". The only way to break the piskey's spell is to take one's coat off, turn it inside out and put it back on again; this will confuse the piskey and the traveller will be able to find the correct path again.

Piskeys also sometimes took horses in the night and rode them to exhaustion, returning them in the morning in no fit state to work. Piskeys could sometimes be diverted or prevented from mischief by gifts, most usually of food; it was once believed that leaving a dish of cream out for the piskeys each night would prevent them from curdling the butter.

There are occasional tales of piskeys or Cornish fairies taking human children for their own. This could be prevented by leaving charms in the crib or even by pinning the child's nightgown to the sides of the bed, but one story tells of a child who was saved by his mother's neglect. This infant was often left at home in the family cottage by his feckless mother, with only the household cat as his guardian. He was also dirty and unwashed; his mother told anyone who asked that the extra layer of dirt kept him warm.

One day the mother returned home to find both cat and baby missing. Searches of the home and surrounding area were fruitless, and all believed that the piskeys had taken the child. The following morning, however, the cat returned and led the mother to a furze bush some distance away, wherein she found her baby, fed, clean and clothed in beautiful garments. The local theory was that the piskeys had planned to take the child with them to their hidden homeland, but it had taken them so long to clean and dress him that they had been surprised by the coming of the dawn and were forced to leave him behind, whereupon the faithful cat effected his rescue.

An old Cornish cottage near Keynance Cove.
iStock

Spriggans were a rather more warlike breed of fairies, who were usually thought to be the guardians of hidden treasure such as might be found in enchanted hills, burial mounds, cairns or barrows. Spriggans inhabited these places, and could sometimes be seen emerging in great numbers if they believed their treasure was threatened. The spriggans of the Gump, near St Just, once attacked a human intruder and immobilised him by pinning his hair to the ground. He only escaped when dawn broke and the spriggans had to return to their hiding places. Meanwhile, miners coming off shift and walking home from Ballowal Mine near St Just reported seeing lights burning and spriggans dancing at Carn Gloose long barrow.

Cornwall is rich in giant-lore, perhaps because of its great numbers of stone circles and other megalithic monuments, the construction of which early settlers attributed to some long-dead race of gargantuan folk. One giant inhabited the Giant's Castle, an Iron Age promontory fort on St Mary's in in the Isles of Scilly. Meanwhile the Giant's Hedge near Lerrin is a seven-mile earthwork supposedly constructed by a giant named Jack, perhaps to mark the boundary of his territory.

There are many putative giants' graves in Cornwall. In fact these are often long barrows or other tumuli, although an 11-foot-long coffin was once unearthed at Tregony, a village between Truro and St Austell. In it was the mouldered skeleton of a man of enormous size, although the bones crumbled to dust on exposure to the air and nothing now remains of this Cornish giant.

Cornish giants were apparently fond of games — many boulders and rock outcrops are thought to be the poorly-aimed results of their games of throw and catch. Indeed, they were particularly fond of quoits; the stone-built chamber tombs at Lanyon and Trevethy

Lanyon Quoit – King Arthur's dining table?

are named after this giantish pastime. Lanyon Quoit was also said to have been used as a dining table by King Arthur and his knights – presumably after the giants had helpfully set it up for them.

The giant Cormoran lived on St Michael's Mount, building it out of white rock which had to be brought from a great distance. His wife Cormelian assisted him, but got tired of fetching the white rock from so far away; instead she decided to use local greenstone, but Cormoran noticed and kicked her in his anger, causing her to drop the greenstone she was carrying. To this day it still rests on the causeway which leads to the Mount, and is known as Chapel Rock.

Cormelian and Cormoran lived peacefully on St Michael's Mount for many years, but one day she was accidentally killed when a giant living on a hill some three miles away threw a hammer to Cormoran, who wanted to borrow it. Cormelian was dazzled by the sun and stumbled, knocking Cormoran out of the way as the hammer flew towards them; it struck her square between the eyes, killing her outright.

Cormoran was grief-stricken by the death of his wife; he buried her deep under the rock of the Mount, but he struggled to recover from his loss. From that day on he became more and more reclusive and bad-tempered, and eventually became something of a menace to the surrounding area, raiding local farms for cattle and sheep to eat. The original legend of Jack the Giant Killer originated here – Jack was a resourceful lad, a farmer's son who got fed up of losing cows to the hungry giant and vowed to solve the problem. He dug a pit on the path leading to Cormoran's lair, covered it with brushwood and then blew his horn, whereupon Cormoran rushed down from the Mount and fell in. After a tremendous battle Jack eventually despatched the giant with a blow from his pickaxe, and then filled in the pit, burying Cormoran's body where it lay.

Another grumpy and troublesome giant named Bolster once fell in love with a local girl, but he was tricked by her into trying to fill a hole in the cliffs near Chapel Porth with his own blood. However, unbeknown to him the hole led directly to the sea, and Bolster bled out and died. The local girl was both beautiful and holy, and a nearby village went on to be named for her – St Agnes, which still celebrates Bolster Day in May each year.

The cliffs near Chapel Porth, where Bolster was tricked and died.
iStock

POOLS, RIVERS AND OTHER WATER SOURCES

Cornwall is a county inextricably linked with water. It is surrounded along three sides by the sea, and even its landward border with neighbouring Devon is marked by a river, the Tamar, which flows south from Woolley Moor, only three and a half miles from the

The rocks and lighthouse off Land's End. Can you hear the bells of lost Lyonesse?
iStock

north Cornish coast, to join the Hamoaze and flow into the sea at Plymouth Sound. King Athelstan fixed the Tamar as the Cornish border in the year 936 and it has remained so almost consistently ever since, making Cornwall into an island in all but name.

Lyonesse

The lost land of Lyonesse is a persistent and poignant legend. It was once, we are told, a prosperous, fertile and beautiful country beyond Land's End stretching out towards the Isles of Scilly, with numerous towns, villages and churches. Its most famous king was called Tristan, and he was brave, noble and renowned throughout the land as a fair and just ruler.

However, one dreadful night (some say it was around 1099) Lyonesse was swallowed by the sea when a freak storm brought a ruinously high tide. Only one man escaped; his name was Trevillian, and when he saw the waves approaching he leaped onto his swiftest horse and galloped bareback ahead of the encroaching tide. By the last few yards of their mad dash the horse was forced to swim through the crashing waves, but they finally gained high ground at Perranuthnoe in the barest nick of time. Fishermen to the south and west of Land's End tell of household goods appearing in their nets, and there are many tales of church bells sounding from the sea as well as ruined walls, towers and buildings occasionally visible at low tide.

Holy Wells

Cornwall's many saints often gave their blessings and magical powers to wells, which have gone on to gather reputations for curative powers or the ability to grant wishes. Lady's Well near Mevagissey is known to have healing properties, while St Non's Well in Altarnun could cure the insane – but only if they were ducked until they were almost unconscious. Water from Madron Well once cured a man who had been crippled since he was a child, while the waters of Bodmin Well had prophetic powers.

Another well, in the village of Constantine Bay near Padstow, is associated with St Constantine, and its waters are said to bring rain during dry weather. Baptism in Ludgvan Well was said to be a sure protection against death by hanging – so it naturally caused some consternation when this fate befell a woman from the parish. However, further investigation showed that in fact she had been baptised in the neighbouring parish, to much relief in Ludgvan.

LEGENDS & FOLKLORE OF CORNWALL

A holy well in a Cornish churchyard.
iStock

Of course, some wells may have had less sanctified properties. St Keyne's Well, near the village of St Keyne not far from Liskeard, was blessed by the saint as she lay dying – apparently, she gave it the power to grant mastery to whoever was the first of a married couple to drink from it. One can only imagine the unseemly races as newly married couples ran from the nearby church to the well on their wedding day. Finally, an old story tells of a well in Sithney, near Helston, whose waters had the reputation of turning women barren. Apparently women would travel from far and wide to drink from it – until the local parson found out and had the well filled in.

Creatures of the Sea

Tales of spirits and creatures of the sea are common around Cornwall – superstitious fishermen once appeased them by making offerings of a few silver fish thrown back from their catches. The most common legendary creature of the ocean is of course the mermaid – or "merrymaid", in Cornwall. Some were friendly – one visited the local church in Zennor and fell in love with the bellringer, a handsome young man named Mathy. He was responsible not only for ringing the church bell before services, but also for tolling it to warn fishermen of approaching storms.

Mathy fell in love with the mermaid, too, and eventually they left together. Neither of them were ever seen in the area again and the local people assumed that she had taken the young man to live with her beneath the waves.

One night some months later the villagers were awoken by the tolling of a great deep bell. When they went to the church the bell there was silent and still, but the tolling continued, calling all the local fishermen safely home. A few hours later a terrible storm blew in, and the villagers thanked God for their deliverance.

However, it seemed that someone else was responsible. A sea captain visited the village a few days later, telling anyone who would listen that he had anchored his ship in St Ives Bay to wait out the recent storm. As the wind and waves were dying away he heard a voice calling from the sea. Looking over the ship's rail he saw a mermaid, who asked him to move his anchor. Apparently it was blocking her doorway, and she was anxious that her husband Mathy would not be able to get in when he returned home from ringing the last bell of Lyonesse to keep the residents of Zennor safe from the storm. In memory of their escape the residents of Zennor caused the image of the mermaid to be carved onto a bench-end in the church; she can still be seen there today.

The Zennor mermaid.

iStock

Another mermaid fell in love with a fisherman named Lutey, who found her stranded on the sand after a high tide and helped her back to the sea. She tried to persuade him to stay with her in the ocean, but he refused, preferring to remain with his wife and chldren on land. In return for rescuing her she gave him her pearled comb, and bestowed on him powers to break curses and evil spells and to heal the sick. She also granted that neither he nor his descendants would ever suffer poverty.

She was a jealous mistress, however, and after nine years she returned to the bay where Lutey lived. She waited until he went out fishing in his boat and then raised the seas, swamping the small craft and washing Lutey overboard. Nevertheless, the story tells that he was not altogether unwilling; the last his shipmates saw of him was as he disappeared into the depths locked in an embrace with his mermaid love.

Some mermaids were not so benign, however; one who lived in the sea near Looe was offended by a local man, so she blocked the harbour and caused the settlement to lose its status as a prosperous port. Another once apparently attracted the attention of a young man of Padstow, but when she rejected his advances he shot and killed her. As she died she cursed him and the town of Padstow, and that night a storm blew up and created the Doom Bar, a giant sandbar that blocked the former deepwater channel that had allowed access to the harbour, with the consequence that large shipping could no longer access the port.

A relatively recent maritime legend is the tale of the Morgawr, a sea monster which allegedly lives in the waters near Falmouth Bay, although it has also been reported on the Atlantic coast of the county. Described as black or grey, sinuous, with a dog-like head and shaped like a serpent or crocodile, local fishermen apparently blame bad weather and poor catches on the monster's presence in the area; there are still occasional sightings of the Morgawr around the Cornish coast.

The huge numbers of wrecks and drownings in Cornish waters have inevitably given rise to tales of ghostly ships and the voices of long-dead mariners, which often call to foretell the coming of a storm or to foreshadow death at sea. A ghostly lady can sometimes be seen sitting on a rock in Sennen Cove. She was the sole survivor of an Irish ship wrecked in a storm, somehow climbing to apparent safety on the rock. However, the seas were too dangerous for the locals to attempt a rescue, and they were forced to watch the lady from the shore as she gradually weakened and was eventually lost to the sea. Her body washed up a few days later, but the rock is named for her; it is still known as the Irish Lady.

A storm at Sennen Cove.
iStock

At Porthcurno there are tales of a ghostly ship with black sails, which was said to belong to a stranger who came to live in the village with his odd and taciturn servant and a pack of wild hounds. Together the two men would take the black ship out of the harbour in the early mornings and return late at night, but no one knew what their business was — most assumed they were privateers or smugglers.

When the stranger died his body was taken to St Levan churchyard and laid in a grave, but when the first clod of earth landed on the coffin the servant and hounds vanished without trace. Ever since then the black ship is said to appear and travel the length of the harbour towards the beach, continuing on its course over dry land up the valley towards St Levan. Eventually it vanishes, but it brings omens of death and misfortune to any who see it.

MINING, FISHING AND OTHER OCCUPATIONS

Tin, copper and silver working has a history dating back at least 2500 years in Cornwall, although the metal mining industry has been in decline for many decades. Metals from Cornwall were bought and sold across Europe and beyond, with the Romans being particularly enthusiastic customers; tin was traded from an offshore isle known as Ictis, thought to be the modern-day St Michael's Mount.

The discovery of tin in Cornwall is attributed to St Piran (he of the floating millstone which carried him across the sea from Ireland). In order to prepare a meal one day Piran constructed a fireplace from the local black stone, but was amazed when white molten metal began to pour from the stone as it heated up. The local villagers were overjoyed at their new source of income, and tin extraction in Cornwall was born.

Like miners everywhere, Cornish tin miners were a superstitious breed. Whistling or swearing underground were frowned upon, and some animals were never called by their proper names – foxes were "'long tails", cats were "rookers" and rats were "peeps". Snails and spiders were thought to bring bad and good luck respectively. A miner who forgot something would never return to fetch it, believing that bad luck would follow him back into the mine if he did so.

Wheal Coates Mine, between Porthtowan and St Agnes.
iStock

Knockers or nuggies were spirits who lived underground and inhabited mine workings, as well as caves and old wells. Miners were generally afraid of them, although sometimes their presence in a mine, announced by the sounds of their knocks and taps as they worked, was taken as a good omen for a rich strike. However, they could be mean and spiteful if their wishes were not honoured; one miner who refused to leave some of his fuggan (currant cake) for the knockers was almost killed by a small cave-in. He narrowly escaped, but he did not learn his lesson and still refused to leave a gift for the spirits – and when he returned to his workings the next morning he found his tools and his pile of ore all buried in a rockfall. Bad luck continued to pursue him until eventually he gave up and sought work as a farm labourer – a terrible fate for a mining man.

Many superstitions were shared between miners and fishermen; indeed, many families had connections with both occupations, and some men even followed them both, going to sea in fine weather and underground in bad. Cornish fishermen never notice or mention rabbits, a parson on the quayside is a bad omen, and churches are always referred to obliquely as "bell houses".

You are never more than twenty-five miles from the sea in Cornwall, and like tin and copper mining, the fishing industry has a long history in the county. Cornish pilchards once provided a staple diet as well as income for many coastal towns and villages, with the launching of the pilchard fleet a whole-town affair once the silvery shoals had been sighted offshore.

Cornish sailors travelled the globe, and were often away for years on end, leaving their sweethearts, wives and families to cope alone. Not all returned safely; a romantic legend from Porthgwarra, near Land's End, tells the tale of Nancy, the daughter of a rich farmer,

The fishing fleet in Newquay harbour.
iStock

and her sailor sweetheart William. Nancy's parents disapproved of their relationship, but they were steadfast and met in secret. Just before William's ship sailed on a long voyage, he and Nancy vowed they would be true to each other and would marry on his return.

Months and then years passed with no word from William, but Nancy refused all other suitors, much against her parents' wishes. Each day she waited at Hella Point for a sign or sight of his ship, but none came, and eventually her heart broke and grief drove her mad.

Confined at home, she took to her bed, but was awoken one night by a dream of William's voice calling to her. She rose and walked to the cove at Porthgwarra, where (it is said) a young man suddenly appeared at her side and took her into his arms. Together the couple walked into the waves and disappeared — and the following morning news arrived in the village that William's ship had been almost home, but had foundered that same night, with all hands.

Porthgwarra Cove, where Nancy and William met for the final time.
iStock

Smugglers

Apart from fishing, Cornwall's other great maritime professions existed on the wrong side of the law. Salvage and smuggling were both viewed as honourable sources of income by those who engaged in them, although the King's Revenue Men did not agree. Any ships which ran aground on Cornish beaches were regarded as fair game; indeed, most people believed they had a right to the pickings that came ashore, and many a family must have been saved from poverty by these gifts from the sea.

Stories exist of Cornishmen wrecking ships on purpose by showing lights and luring them onto rocks; the most infamous wrecker, a Dane named David Coppinger, may well have done this. However, such events are likely to have been few and far between; the more usual response to a wreck off the coast would have been fearless

courage in the face of wild seas to save both men and goods from the waves, since the Cornish are a seafaring people themselves and know the dangers only too well.

However, smuggling was rife, with the smuggling men (or "free traders") having an honour and brotherhood all their own. Spirits, tobacco, spices and other goods were bought cheaply on the Continent and then brought ashore on isolated Cornish beaches and hidden before being moved on for sale in Bristol and London. Many Cornish coves and isolated pubs, farms and even churches have a smuggling history, and fabulous riches were shared among all those who took part in the landing, concealment and onward transport of the contraband goods. Jamaica Inn, remote and isolated on Bodmin Moor, is these days well known as an erstwhile smuggling inn; it even has its own smuggling museum, along with a collection of resident ghosts.

The Revenue Men in their scarlet jackets were kept busy, with violent clashes and deaths not uncommon. The possible penalties for being caught smuggling including imprisonment, transportation to Australia and even hanging. However, the redcoats were often outsmarted, and sometimes became targets themselves — and even when smugglers were brought to trial the juries (usually composed of local men who may well have been involved in the free trade themselves, since most people were) often found them innocent.

Jamaica Inn on Bodmin Moor, once the haunt of smugglers.
Neil Howard

Smuggling was a vital source of income for many households, and in some areas almost everyone, from landowners down to the meanest and most poverty-stricken unemployed miners, was likely to have been involved at some level. Legend has it that Talland parish church, on the clifftops above Looe Bay, is so situated because the builders eventually gave in to nocturnal meddlers who kept moving their stones from their intended site in the village to the site above the bay. A supernatural explanation was suggested, but it seems more likely that smugglers wanted a clifftop location in order to be able to signal to ships out at sea.

SUPERSTITIONS AND OMENS

The uncertainty and precariousness of life in bygone centuries meant that signs, symbols and superstitions were given great importance. Life was ruled by observations and omens, and the closeness of our rural ancestors' relationship with the natural world around them meant that many of these proverbs referred to the behaviour of plants, animals and even the weather – and some were in rhyming form, perhaps to aid the memory. For example:

Hawthorn bloom and elder flowers
Will fill a house with evil powers

When old cats play, rain is on the way

If there's ice in November to hold a duck,
There will be a winter of slush and muck

If the moon on a Saturday be new or full,
There always was rain and there always will.

Onion skins very thin: a mild winter coming in.
Onion skins thick and tough: coming winter wild and rough.

If spiders are many and spinning their webs, the weather will soon be very dry.

When pine cones open on the trees, the weather is set fine.

Oak before ash — we're in for a splash;
Ash before oak — we're in for a soak.

Household activities were set about with superstitions of all kinds. A hat on a bed brought bad luck, while a candle flickering or burning with a blue flame indicated the presence of a spirit in the room. Other proverbs and sayings related to commerce or education (although they may not be taken as the truth nowadays!). For example:

He that buys land buys many stones,
He that buys flesh buys many bones,
He that buys eggs buys many shells,
But he that buys good ale buys nothing else.

A cow, a sow and a woman — you can learn them nothing,
A dog, a horse and a man — you can learn them anything.

The harvesting of certain crops was thought to be related to the phase of the moon, as shown in this rhyme:

When the moon is at the full,
Mushrooms you may freely pull;
But when the moon is on the wane,
Wait 'ere you think to pluck again.

Good Luck, Bad Luck

According to our rural ancestors, if you want to avoid bad luck for yourself or someone else you should avoid doing the following:

Walking under a ladder

Putting shoes or boots on the table

Shaking hands across the dinner table

Spilling salt on the table

Singing at the table

Sleeping on the table

Placing your knife and fork crossways on your plate

Turning your bed on a Sunday

Brushing the dust out of the front door

Giving gloves as a present

Cutting your fingernails on a Monday, Friday or Sunday

Opening an umbrella in the house

Bringing thyme into the house

Carrying anything on your shoulder in the house

Entering a house for the first time through the back door

Throwing dead flowers onto the fire

Cutting down a flowering tree

Turning back after beginning a journey

Doing anything on Friday 13th

Nailing up a horseshoe with the points down (all the luck will drain out)

Killing a sparrow (they carry the souls of the dead)

Breaking a mirror

Treading on a grave

Leaving a house by a different door from the one you used to enter

Giving a gift of an empty purse or wallet (it should always contain a little money)

Likewise, to ensure good luck you should:

Carry a piece of coal in your pocket
Carry a piece of iron with a hole in it
Carry a rabbit's foot
Keep a lock of hair from a baby's first haircut
Burn your tea leaves
Salute a solitary magpie
Wish on a falling star
Bow nine times to the new moon
Cut your fingernails on a Thursday
Put on your left sock or stocking first when getting dressed
Pick up a pin if you see one
Pick up a white stone, spit on it and throw it over your head
Take a snail by its horns and throw it backwards over your shoulder
Throw a pinch of salt over your left shoulder
Begin a journey with your right foot first
Look for a four-leaved clover
Look for a double-leaved sprig of ash
If you see a penny or a pin on the ground, always pick it up

Let a black cat cross your path

Nail up a horseshoe with the points upwards (to keep the luck from spilling out — and always use seven nails!)

Cross your fingers if you accidentally do anything unlucky

Catch a falling leaf — the more you catch, the more good luck you will have

Sunset on a Cornish beach.
iStock

THE JOURNEY THROUGH LIFE

Life was more precarious in the past. A lack of understanding as to the cause of diseases or the knowledge of how to cure them meant mortality rates were high, especially among children. For the same reason, accidents involving injury were also far more serious. Wars were more frequent, too.

The perilous journey through life had important stages which were celebrated with ritual and accompanied by superstition. There were several strange beliefs regarding the beginning of life. It was said that a child born at midnight would have second sight, and that a "footling" – that is, a baby born feet first – would have magical powers. Efforts were made to preserve the caul surrounding the child at birth because it was thought to be possessed with sympathetic magic. Kept safe, it would prevent the person it belonged to from suffering death by drowning. There are records from well into the twentieth century of sailors buying cauls in the belief they would keep them safe.

As soon as a woman went into labour, a party called a Merry Meet would be held at her house. The prospective father would entertain family and neighbours, and a "groaning cheese" and a "groaning cake" would be carefully cut into exactly the right number of pieces to serve to the guests; it was regarded as the height of bad manners to refuse a piece. Unfortunately, of course, the woman giving birth was unable to enjoy the festivities herself.

With infant mortality so high, it was considered essential to christen a newborn baby as soon as possible. An unbaptised child would not go to heaven if they died, and some thought they might become fairies instead. Some measure of protection could be conferred on the infant by wrapping it in its mother's clothes until the baptism could take place, or by tying a red string about its wrist. While the child was still unbaptised it was customary to make them a gift of an egg (symbolising new life), some salt and, unsafe though it may seem, a box of matches. Salt and fire were considered sure charms against the attentions of evil spirits.

A Christening custom from Cornwall was the fuggan, or large currant cake, which was baked for the celebrations. A piece of the cake known as the kimbly was cut and carried in the Christening procession on the way to church, and was presented to the first person met along the road. If this person accepted the morsel, the child being christened would be safe from the supernatural (particularly the mischievous Cornish piskeys) for the rest of its life.

If the baptism was performed at home the water used to christen the child was often thrown into the fire, to ensure it remained pure and no evil influence could pollute it. Even after baptism the infant might be at risk from fairies, who were thought to cast acquisitive eyes at human children. To ward them off, parents might hang a pair of scissors or tongs over the crib, which would dangle in the form of a cross. The cross shape and the iron in the scissors were sure protection against the little people.

If fairies did get their hands on a baby they would leave in its place a changeling, a peevish and ugly fairy child, or a block of wood enchanted to resemble the stolen infant. Babies who succumbed to what we now call Sudden Infant Death Syndrome (SIDS, or cot death) were often thought to be the lifeless substitutes left behind by kidnapping fairies.

Some mothers would bite their children's fingernails short rather than cutting them, in the belief that if they cut the fingernails the child would grow up to be a thief. It was also said that a new baby must always be carried upstairs before it goes down, otherwise it would not rise in life. If there were no stairs in the house, the midwife would climb onto a chair with it.

New mothers feared their children might be stolen by fairies unless they protected them with charms until they were baptised.

In young adulthood, there were also some interesting customs surrounding courtship. We tend to assume morals were more conservative in the past, so it may be a surprise to learn that courting couples were often allowed to sleep together undisturbed. However, this was only with the proviso that the young man kept his clothes on (minus his coat and boots). A variant custom called "bundling" allowed the couple to share a bed with a bolster between them. Such would have been the disgrace if the young couple abused this trust that few did. Mind you, engagements tended to be shorter in those days.

In Cornwall the rural villages were sometimes so insular and isolated that marrying someone from outside the settlement was thought of as a crime. One story tells of a man seeking a wife from a neighbouring town who was 'arrested' by his neighbours and brought back home in a wheelbarrow — presumably still single.

A young woman hoping to marry into a farming family was often called upon to prove her strength by lifting the lid of the parish chest with one arm. The parish chest was an ancient and massive locked casket kept in the church, which was used to store charitable donations and other valuables. It was usually made of thick oak, sometimes carved out of one solid piece of wood, and was usually bound with stout iron. To lift its heavy lid with one arm would be quite a feat for many men, never mind a young woman.

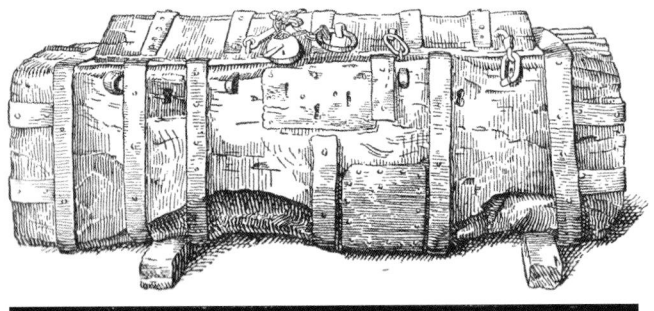

A parish chest.

As to the wedding day itself, there was an ancient custom in which the friends of the groom would call at the bride's house with a view to "abducting" her. Her duty was to hide, so as to avoid this indignity, or — better still — to sneak to the church before they caught her. This was a remnant of a much older custom in which young men would prove their worth by stealing the girl they fancied from under her parents' roof. In more civilised times, no abduction or manhandling of the bride actually took place and the whole thing was done in fun.

A rather unkind superstition related to weddings was that if a woman served as a bridesmaid three times, she would never be married herself. Likewise, a man who acted as best man three times would never wed. But there are even stranger beliefs; for example, if a young woman puts on a man's hat or a young man puts on a woman's hat, they will have to wait three years before they can get married. If a young person cuts bread obliquely or in uneven slices they will never be married, they may have to wait seven years, or else they will end up with an objectionable mother-in-law. If a girl touches the foot of another girl with a broom while sweeping, she will rob that girl of her future husband. Finally, when the bride enters the church, she must never look behind her or she will end up regretting the marriage.

There are equally strange superstitions regarding the final great change in a person's life – death. Dogs howling or owls screeching might be taken as omens of a coming death. Clocks suddenly stopping or chiming thirteen were a bad sign, as were a robin tapping at the window pane, a crow getting into the house or an owl settling on the roof. Mysterious noises such as knocks and raps in a house where someone lay ill were also ominous. Carpenters sometimes claimed they heard sounds in their workshops at night resembling those of a coffin being made. They knew then that one would soon be ordered.

When the last moment seemed to be nigh, people were sometimes "helped to die" by those looking after them. All the doors and windows in the house were opened wide to allow the soul to escape. At the same time, knots were untied, mirrors covered and the fire – the "soul of the house" – was put out. "Passing bells" were traditionally rung nine times to announce a death, but their original purpose was to scare away any evil spirits seeking to claim the soul of the departed. A plate of salt, a substance long believed to ward off evil, was placed on the body. No corpse was left with its eyes open, for it was said that it would be looking for the next person to die.

After a death, the household would keep watch for at least one night while the corpse lay in the house because it was thought that the soul of the departed might return. Sometimes the assembly would chant, "It is for the last time, it is the last night", in order to remind the spirit that it had to pass on. If the master of the house died it was considered important to inform the bees in the hive of the fact, otherwise they would all fly away. Any significant tree or bush, even household plants, were at one time draped with black crêpe after a death, otherwise it was feared they would wither.

When the corpse was conveyed to its burial place it had to be taken to its grave in the same direction as the sun passes through the sky – that is, "deosil" or clockwise. To take it in the opposite direction, "widdershins" or anti-clockwise, would make the soul vulnerable to malign forces. There was a prejudice about being the first person buried in a new graveyard, because it was said that the Devil had the right to claim the first corpse. Another superstition suggested that the spirit of the most recent person to be buried haunted a graveyard, watching over it until another burial took place.

A decidedly primitive custom, which had all but died out by the end of the nineteenth century, was that of the "sin-eater". The sin-eater was usually a poor member of the parish who was prepared, for a small fee and a meal, to spiritually take on the sins of a person who had just died. This would be achieved by offering them specially baked cakes, or bread on a dish of salt, the eating of which meant that he would absorb the sins. The food might even be offered over the coffin of the dead person; at any rate, the meal would always be eaten in the graveyard. This belief seems to hark back to the time when our most distant ancestors believed they could take on the power and attributes of a deceased person by devouring their body. The sin-eater was therefore a kind of spiritual cannibal.

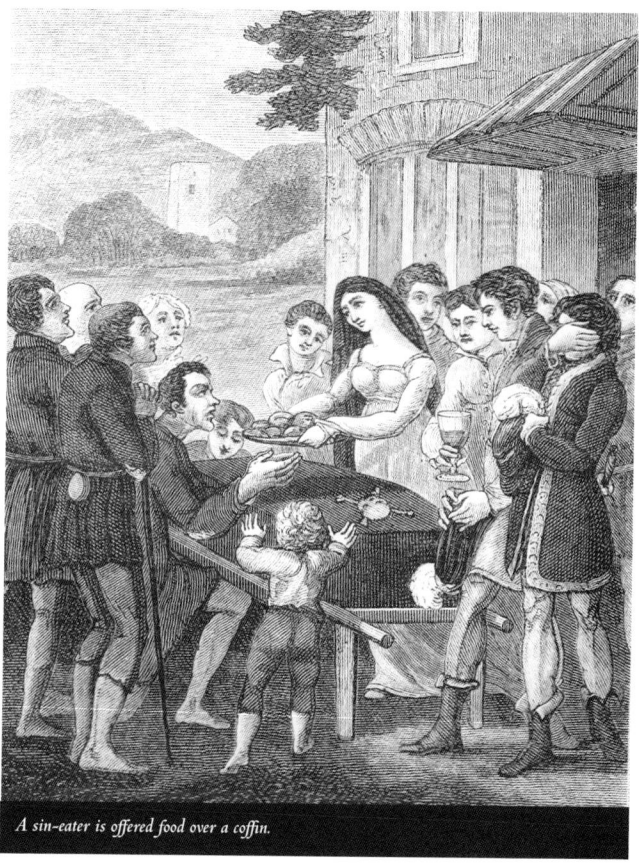

A sin-eater is offered food over a coffin.

THE WHEEL OF THE YEAR

The rural calendar was marked by a series of high days and festivals intended to mark crucial times for sowing, reaping and other agricultural activities. These were often of great antiquity, pre-dating the Christian era. Many were adopted by the church, although rededicated and renamed, and have therefore been preserved down the years.

The Celtic New Year was marked on 1 November, when winter began. The coming dark days were defied with a great celebratory feast called Samhain. Bonfires were lit, animals were mated for the following spring, and any surplus beasts were slaughtered to fatten everyone up in advance of the approaching cold. Guy Fawkes Night is a survival of the Samhain bonfire festival, merely put back a few days and given a political context which would have meant nothing to our pagan ancestors.

As a transitional period between the old year and the new, Samhain was considered a time when spirits from the underworld could revisit the earth. It was a time of ghosts and witches. This ancient belief is recalled in our modern-day Hallowe'en traditions. The church diffused the apparent menace in this festival by dedicating 1 November to all the saints in heaven. Hallows is an archaic word for saints, and Hallowe'en is a contraction of All Hallows Eve – that is, the night before All Hallows or All Saints Day. It was formerly custom around this time to go Soul Caking, roaming the parish in request of small gifts of money to be presented with specially baked dainties called soul cakes. Guisers or mummers also put on plays and entertainments, usually disguised or with their faces blackened.

In Cornwall Hallowe'en used to be called Allantide, a name which may be connected with the old Cornish word *aval*, apple. This fruit and its pips used to be used for divination of various kinds, and it has a seasonal connection with Autumn and the turn of the season into Winter.

The next great festival in the Celtic calendar was Imbolc, on 1 February. This marked the beginning of the lambing season and is echoed in the Christian Feast of the Purification of the Virgin Mary, or Candlemas, celebrated the following day. Candlemas was dedicated to new mothers and childbirth.

The start of summer was celebrated on 1 May, in the Celtic festival called Beltane. Given over to fertility and the reawakening of the earth, this was a free-for-all party, with singing, dancing, the lighting of more bonfires and a certain amount of licence. May Day continued the tradition in a diluted form. Dancing round the maypole, a pretty ritual, probably replaced a more ribald ceremony; in Cornwall maypoles adorn the village greens of many places, but it was once the custom for neighbouring villages to try to steal each other's maypoles. Guards were often set, but opposing villages would resort to sneaky tricks such as getting the guards drunk or letting down the tyres of their vehicles so they couldn't stand their watch. Padstow deserves a special mention because of the famous (and quite sinister) Obby Oss that dances through the streets of the town on 1 May each year, accompanied by singers and musicians, and of course the traditional Floral Dance (or Furry Dance) in Helston takes place in early May – both well worth a visit.

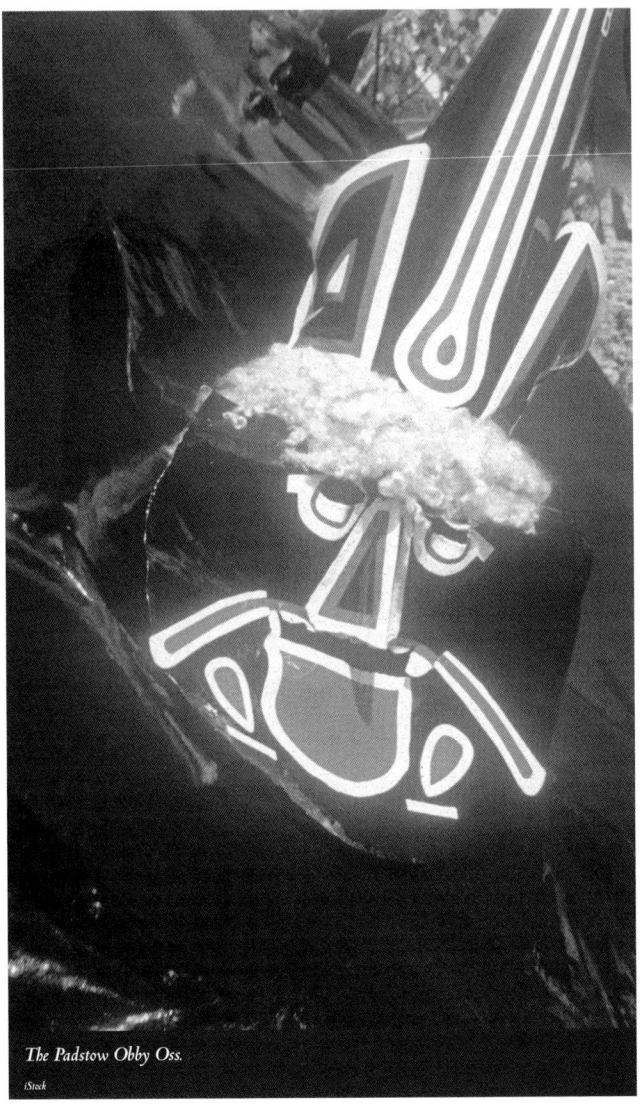
The Padstow Obby Oss.
iStock

The last of the big four Celtic festivals took place on 1 August and was called Lughnasadh. This was the harvest festival, when the grain would be gathered in. The Christianised Saxons knew it as *hlaf-maesse*, meaning "loaf-mass", which later became corrupted to Lammas or Lammastide. In Cornwall the harvest was celebrated in the fields with an ancient ritual; the oldest harvester would cut the final sheaf of standing corn with his scythe, and then would raise the bundle of wheat stalks above his head. He would cry, "I have 'un! I have 'un! I have 'un!" The assembled villagers would reply, "What 'ave ee? What 'ave ee? What 'ave ee?" The harvester would reply, "A neck! A neck! A neck!" A great cheer would go up, and the assembled crowd would return home for a harvest feast.

In between these four seasonal festivals were many others, some pagan and some of Christian origin, and others, like Easter and Christmas, a blend of the two. Lupercalia, the Roman celebration of youth, took place in the middle of February. In the warmer climes of the east it served as something of a harbinger of spring in which young people were encouraged to choose lovers. It had a reputation for excess that was thoroughly defused by the adoption in its place of the feast honouring the martyrdom of St Valentine, which took place on 14 February. Valentine was a gentleman committed to chastity, and it seems his association with romantic love was merely a matter of convenience. Nonetheless, St Valentine's Day remains one of the most popular traditions in the modern calendar, and people have been exchanging love tokens on this day for centuries.

Shrovetide marks the start of Lent, a period of fasting and abstinence leading up to Easter. In modern times we mark Shrove Tuesday by making and eating pancakes, but our rural ancestors marked the start of the fasting season in other ways too. One Shrovetide custom was barring out, when school pupils would barricade their school against the master or mistress and try to prevent them from entering, often for a period of days. If they were successful they won the right to games or a holiday, but if the master managed to gain entry to the school he imposed extra lessons as punishment. This tradition was once widespread but had died out in most places by the turn of the century.

Although Easter honours the crucifixion and resurrection of Christ, there are many secular traditions attached to it which date from pre-Christian times. It is likely that the name Easter has been borrowed from a pagan goddess of the spring, Eostre. The Easter Bunny may well be a descendant of the hare, an animal associated with the spring and fertility and sacred to the Celts.

Eggs are a natural symbol of rebirth and were equally appropriate for both the Resurrection and for spring, the season in which Easter falls. It was once a common pastime on Easter Day for people to roll gaily coloured hard-boiled eggs down hillsides in a jovial race. This was called "pace-egging" or "egg-rolling", and it has been suggested that the rolling eggs represented the life-giving sun's passage through the sky, but it was also widely believed that if one's egg reached the bottom of the hill unscathed, good luck would surely follow.

"Lifting" was a widespread and peculiar custom, which was once carried out at Easter but has now died out. It took place on Easter Monday and Tuesday. A chair would be garlanded with flowers and people would take it in turns to sit in it while their fellows raised them into the air. It was common for men to lift women on Easter Monday and the other way round on Easter Tuesday, with the lifters claiming kisses and sometimes money as their rewards. A pleasant performance in the villages, it could be a rowdy affair in towns, where strangers were sometimes bundled into the chair and forced to pay a fee in order to be let down again. In all locations, however, the lifting ceased promptly at noon.

Other traditions relating to Easter are unarguably Christian, however. On Good Friday, the day of Christ's Crucifixion, we still eat hot cross buns. At one time it was common for all loaves to be marked

The archaic custom of lifting was popular on Easter Monday and the following Tuesday but has now completely died out.

with a cross. Despite its name, Good Friday's association made it an unlucky day in the minds of our ancestors. It has become a bank holiday because those engaged in dangerous occupations, such as mining and fishing, refused to work on that day. Blacksmiths and those in the building trades would often down tools too, because it was considered poor taste to handle nails on that day.

Easter itself was quite different in character. Easter Sunday was always given over to worship, while Easter Monday was a holiday for leisure and sports. Some believed that the sun danced on Easter Sunday in joyous memory of the resurrection, and it was formerly a custom to rise before dawn in the hope of seeing this phenomenon. It was also traditional to wear new clothes on Easter Sunday, or at least one item that had never been worn before.

Beating the bounds was another ritual commonly carried out at this time of the year, usually on Ascension Day (5 May). In the days before maps were freely available, it was important to clearly define parish boundaries and to ensure that nothing had occurred to alter them. Beating the bounds was sometimes taken rather too literally, however. The villagers, accompanied by a clergyman, would take the young boys of the parish on a tour of the landmarks on its boundary. At each one they would pause and the boys would be whipped to make sure they remembered them.

The day before the feast of St John the Baptist, or St John's Eve, falls on 23 June. It was also known as Midsummer Eve, even though the summer solstice – the longest day of the year – falls a couple of days before. Once again, this important stage in the year was celebrated with the lighting of bonfires. There were also numerous customs and celebrations associated with the bringing in of the harvest in the autumn, and traditional fairs and sales were held at Michaelmas, on 29 September.

The final great festival of the winter was, of course, Christmas. There is in fact no biblical reference to the date of Christ's birthday, and 25 December was chosen because it coincided with ancient pagan rituals associated with the winter solstice, the shortest day of the year, and with the birth dates of rival gods such as Mithras – 25 December became the Festival of the Unconquered Sun during the reign of the Roman Emperor Aurelius. It made sense for the early Christians to adopt a day already given over to celebration, especially one relating to the sense of hope engendered by the start of longer days and shorter nights.

Many of the old traditional customs associated with Christmas are of pre-Christian origin. Prince Albert, Queen Victoria's husband, is famously credited with bringing the custom of decorating a fir tree to Britain from his native Germany. In fact, there are records of an evergreen tree lit with candles being set up in a London street as long ago as the fifteenth century. This seems to have been a Norse tradition, as was the selecting of a Yule log, although the word "Yule" is Anglo-Saxon in origin.

The lighting of fires was a central element to the ancient Celtic celebrations. Fire gave warmth and light, allowed food to be cooked and represented that great life-bringer, the sun. Fire therefore brought luck and scared away the powers of darkness. The Yule log would be selected with great ceremony and celebration, in much the way we would choose a Christmas tree today. The larger the fireplace, the larger the log chosen to fill it. Lighting the log traditionally took place on Christmas Eve, ideally from a saved fragment from the previous year, and if it was big enough the log might bring warmth throughout Christmas Day and beyond.

Holly became associated with Christmas because it is an evergreen, and mistletoe simply because it was the plant most sacred to our

Celtic ancestors. According to a Roman historian, the druids would only allow mistletoe to be cut with a golden sickle as it was so precious.

Cutting and bringing home the Yule log was a major occasion in big houses during the run up to Christmas.
iStock

The Twelve Days of Christmas, which included our present New Year's Day and Twelfth Night (6 January), were the perfect excuse for having a good time. Where possible, big family gatherings would be held or feasts where the servants as well as the masters would be entertained. Carols would be sung by the poor, and extra pennies collected to help them celebrate later on. A more boisterous variant on carol singing was the traditional wassailing. Wassail is an old English word meaning "be of good cheer". Poor people would walk round the parish singing wassailing songs either for money or, more usually, beer. Those who were better off might have in their possession a wassail cup, large and often of elaborate design, which they would fill with mulled beer or wine and use to toast each other. In Truro the wassailers visited pubs and householders in the town, begging for money, food and drink and repaying benefactors with the following blessing:

Now we poor wassail boys are weary and cold,
Drop a small piece of silver into our bowl.
We hope that your apple trees will prosper and bear,
And bring forth good cider when we come next year!

Mummers' plays – medieval morality plays – were also performed in many places. In a custom dating back to Roman times, the roles of master and servant were overturned on one day of the year around Christmas time, with the staff served a feast by their employers. Sometimes a Lord of Misrule might be appointed from among the servants – a kind of fool king. In some military regiments even today the officers serve Christmas dinner to their men. Another custom was to lay the table for two on Christmas Eve, to welcome Joseph and Mary on Christmas morning. There was also a superstition that animals were able to talk on Christmas morning, and some people, particularly children, would creep to the pens and cowsheds as the sun rose in the hope of catching them doing so.

It was generally considered that using scissors on New Year's Day would bring bad fortune. However, the first water drawn from any pond, stream or well on New Year's Day was traditionally held to be lucky. It was known as the Flower of the Well, and there was often great competition to be the first to reach the water source after the stroke of midnight. If a young woman drew the water she would marry her true love within a twelve-month; if a farmer did so, he would often use it to wash his dairy utensils and then give it to his cattle to drink, to bless them for the year to come. Bottled and kept in a house, it would bring good luck to all who dwelled there.

In Cornwall it was considered unlucky to pay off a debt at New Year, since it would result in a succession of payments throughout the coming year. Nothing must be taken from a house on New Year's Day, but as much as possible brought in, to ensure prosperity for the year ahead. Also, Cornish households took care that the first person to cross the threshold in the New Year should be male, since females brought bad luck in with them. Finally, it was also traditional to celebrate New Year's Day with a party, reflecting the universal belief that it is lucky to begin anything in good spirits. Of course, this tradition still holds true today.

I wish you a happy Christmas and a happy New Year,
A pocket full of money and a cellar full of beer,
And a good fat pig to last you all the year.

Mistletoe, an unusual plant that is a parasite on other trees, is now closely associated with Christmas but at one time it was venerated by the Druids.
iStock

A CORNISH MISCELLANY

Some believe Cornwall to be named after Corineus, a hero who was given the south west peninsula of Britain as his estate after defeating the giant Gogmagog in a wrestling match on Plymouth Hoe. However, it is more likely to have been named for the Cornovii, the Roman name for the Iron Age tribe who lived in the area, with '-wall' indicating the Old English word for foreigner or stranger (Wales is thought to take its name from the same root).

It is one of the most geographically and culturally distinct of the English counties. For all but four miles of the county border it is separated from Devon by the physical boundary of the River Tamar, making it almost island-like, but it is also set apart by its culture, heritage and even by its language. The old Cornish language, Kernewek, is a Brythonic Celtic language like Welsh and Breton, but it died out as a first language in the 18th century, possibly because of the lack of a printed body of literature but likely also influenced by the demise of the tin-mining industry and associated mass emigration.

However, Kernewek is currently experiencing a revival. It is now recognised as an important part of Cornish regional culture, identity and heritage, and is increasingly taught in schools in Cornwall. There are rising numbers of bilingual speakers of English and Cornish, and it is offered as an adult education course in locations both inside and outside Cornwall. There is a well-known couplet:

By tre, pol and pen,
You shall know the Cornishmen

These three words, tre (homestead), pol (lake) and pen (headland), occur in many old Cornish place names and personal names, and are some of the best known and most recognisable survivals from Kernewek.

Looking out to Rumps Point.
iStock

As well as their independence and fierce local pride, Cornish people are also known for their thrift. A story from the Bodmin Moor area tells of a farmer who lost his right leg in an agricultural accident. A few months later a friend of his went to war and lost his left leg in battle. Both survived their injuries, and went on to live harmoniously as neighbours, buying a pair of boots between them every year.

Cornwall has two national sports – Cornish wrestling, and hurling. Cornish wrestling has a long history; it was recorded by Geoffrey of Monmouth around 1139 that Corineus, the legendary ruler of Cornwall, wrestled the giant Gogmagog. The sport has a standardised rules system; wrestlers wear heavy jackets and the object is to grip and throw the opponent, with umpires known as sticklers and a points system deciding the winner of the bout. It features at the Royal Cornwall Show, as well as in matches with the county's great rival, Devon.

Meanwhile, Cornish hurling is a game played with a small silver ball, similar to traditional mass football games played elsewhere in the country (notably Ashbourne in Derbyshire). The most notable example these days takes place in St Columb Major, happening on Shrove Tuesday and again eleven days later. The object is for each team (which can have any number of members; games often involve all the men in a parish, and may even take place between parishes) to carry the ball to their own goal or over the parish boundary. The game can range anywhere in a town, and the winning team is the first to goal the ball. Traditionally the winning player gets to keep the ball, but must provide another one for the next game – and since they are made of applewood encased in silver and may cost a substantial amount to replace, many hurling balls have been in use for a number of years.

Of course, no visit to Cornwall would be complete without sampling a pasty. The county's signature dish was traditionally the portable food of miners, with the filling of beef, swede and onion kept safe and succulent by the golden crimped pastry case, ready to be reheated if necessary on a shovel over a candle. Sometimes known as 'oggies' in Cornwall, these days the beef pasty has protected geographical status as the only true Cornish version, but in days gone by they were likely to have been made with whatever meat was available – perhaps giving rise to the old saying that the Devil was afeared to cross the Tamar into Cornwall, for fear he'd end up in a pasty!

Another of Cornwall's delicacies is the famous starry-gazy pie – a tasty fish pie traditionally made with pilchards, where the fish heads are left protruding through the pastry and gazing upwards. The legend behind the creation of this dish recalls a dreadful winter in the village of Mousehole during the sixteenth century, when the fishermen were unable to leave port for weeks on end. By the time Christmas approached the people were staring starvation in the face.

Eventually one old fisherman, Tom Bawcock, decided he'd rather take his chances on the stormy ocean than die of starvation. He set out from Mousehole harbour into the teeth of a wild tempest, and the people wept to see him go, convinced he would never return. Miraculously, however, he and his craft survived and returned with a huge catch of seven different sorts of fish – the village was saved, and the first starry-gazy pies were baked in celebration, with the pilchards looking to heaven and giving thanks for the village's deliverance. Even today, December 23 is celebrated in Mousehole as Tom Bawcock's Eve.

A Cornish pasty.
iStock

Saffron buns.
iStock

When a Cornish miner or fisherman had eaten his dinner of pasty or fish pie, he might very well have reached for a saffron bun or a slice of fuggan for pudding. Saffron buns are spiced, fruited and flavoured with delicate saffron; they are rich and yellow, and served with butter. Fuggan is a type of dough cake flavoured with raisins – although it might also have been made in a savoury version with meat and potatoes pressed into the dough.

Either way, before his meal any god-fearing Cornish man would have been sure to say grace in the Cornish style: "Lord make us able to eat what's on the table." Replete after finishing his pasty and his slice of fuggan, he might have leaned back in his chair and uttered, "The Lord be praised, our stomachs be aised."

FURTHER READING

There are many works on folklore, myths and legends across the British Isles, some general and some specific to different areas. The following works were useful in the compilation of this book.

A Dictionary of British Folk Customs by Christina Hole
(1976, Helicon)

Albion: A Guide to Legendary Britain by Jennifer Westwood
(1987, Paladin)

Cornish Folk Tales by Mike O'Connor (2010, The History Press)

Cornwall's Strangest Tales by Peter Grego (2013, Portico Books)

Encyclopedia of Traditional British Sports by Tony Collins, John Martin and Wray Vamplew (2005, Psychology Press)

England in Particular by Sue Clifford and Angela King
(2006, Hodder and Stoughton)

Myths and Legends of the British Isles by Richard Barber
(1999, The Boydell Press)

The Folklore of Cornwall by Tony Deane and Tony Shaw
(1975, Batsford)

The Lore of the Land by Jennifer Westwood and Jacqueline Simpson
(2005, Penguin)